Abortio...
Choosing Who Lives

Evaluating the Process
by which Abortion is Permitted

Rick Simpson

Priest in Charge of Holy Trinity, Jesmond and
St. Barnabas and St. Jude, Newcastle

RIDLEY HALL RD CAMBRIDGE CB3 9HU

Contents

Acknowledgments

My thanks to the many people who have discussed the arguments in this booklet with me and offered encouragement, advice and critique, including members of the Grove Ethics Group, especially David Clough and Andrew Goddard, GPs in my congregation, and Andrew Fergusson and Peter Saunders of CMF.

The Cover Illustration is by Peter Ashton

First Impression July 2002
ISSN 1470-854X
ISBN 1 85174 503 3

Why Another Booklet About Abortion?

1

This booklet is a Christian ethical reflection on the process by which abortions are authorized in England and Wales.

It asks what impact this system may have upon our attitudes as a society to pregnancy and children, and how general practitioners are being used or abused when facing abortion requests. Discussions of abortion—in Christian and secular ethics—are often focussed, appropriately enough, on the morality of the act itself. However, the actual *process* by which individuals seek the consent of doctors, operating under the law, to authorize abortions receives less attention.[1] This process itself needs to be analysed and questioned ethically; that is the specific task of this booklet.

The actual process by which individuals seek the consent of doctors receives less attention

Hence I will not be rehearsing the Christian ethical argument against abortion. Similarly, I will not be addressing important questions within the abortion debate—when life begins, the rights of the unborn, cases in which sanctioning abortion might be a legitimate option, and so on. Discussions of these questions and systematic Christian arguments against abortion already exist; I am not seeking to add to these treatments.[2] My argument does however assume a position that I need to state briefly at the outset.

Life is a gift from God, to the child [itself], to parents, and [to] the community

This position is that abortion[3] is, with rare exceptions, a wrongful act, as it constitutes the intentional killing of an unborn child, or at least of a human foetus with full potential to live. Life is a gift from God, to the child itself, to parents, and to the community; once a pregnancy has begun it is simply wrong to deliberately end that life, just as it is wrong to end the life of the newly born, children, adults, or the elderly. All such acts are contrary to God's prohibition on murder and Christ's command to love.

In taking this position I do not suggest that all women who have had an abortion made their decision lightly. On the contrary, behind each abortion lies a story, and many are stories of women who are afraid, unsupported, isolated or deeply divided in themselves about what to do. Part of my argument is about who really is on the side of a woman facing the agonizing decision about whether to continue her pregnancy, and whether abortion serves her best interests. I suggest it does not, and that our abortion process makes it easy for the other characters in each personal drama—especially the father—to evade rather than face their responsibilities, adding to the isolation that many pregnant women feel.

Our abortion process makes it easy for the other characters in each personal drama to evade responsibility

In arguing that abortion is basically wrong I am also not ruling out the possibility of there being 'limit cases' in which it might be justified, nor arguing that all abortion should be illegal. My presumed position accepts that abortion can be justified in the few cases where the mother's life is seriously risked by continuing the pregnancy, and it allows for other possible cases in which it might be argued that abortion is a legitimate choice, for example rape pregnancies, or extreme cases of non-viability in the unborn child.

I cannot discuss these limit cases here. However, having acknowledged room for a reasonable Christian ethical debate in such areas, only 2% of abortions in England and Wales in recent years were permitted on grounds that might fall within such limit cases; it is the other 98% I want to discuss.[4] My argument concerns this huge majority of abortions performed for other reasons, and the process by which they are deemed legal and indeed acceptable.

I believe that the vast majority of Christians who see Scripture as their ultimate authority basically share the ethical position on abortion just outlined; few Protestants of evangelical, charismatic and pentecostal traditions, or practising Roman Catholics would dissent greatly from it.

I also believe this position is widely shared among Christian doctors. Research published by the Christian Medical Fellowship in 1996 showed that a large majority of the Christian doctors surveyed thought that abortion law needed reform, and wanted to see the number of abortions allowed being re-

The process privat choices affecting tl whole of society

duced.[5] However, some of these doctors found it difficult to pursue practice that did justice to their convictions.[6] This is not to suggest that Christian GPs fail to take their convictions to work with them or act according to conscience. On the contrary, they generally take this issue extremely seriously and are profoundly troubled by handling abortion requests.[7] Nevertheless, for many there is clearly some tension between their convictions and the practice they adopt, or feel forced to adopt.

My response here is to question the actual process by which abortions are permitted, and analyse the position GPs (and indeed pregnant mothers) are actually placed in by it. I believe that this process is deeply flawed. It systematically subverts the attempt by GPs to handle abortion requests on a good ethical basis, and privatizes choices affecting the whole of society. I outline and raise questions about this process in Chapter Two. I will argue that most abortions are authorized only because the supposedly medical criteria by which they are permitted are simply unspecified. Doctors are cautious about saying that cases fall outside the lines because it is completely unclear where those lines lie.

In Chapter Three I offer some reflections on the ethical implications of this process. I will argue that our current process has resulted in us often treating pregnancy, functionally, as an illness, for which there is a cure. It allows us to believe that value or rights are conferred upon unborn children not according to any worth they have as human beings or (better) members of our community, but strictly according to the mother's private choice. I compare this with the high valuation of the unborn in other situations in our culture, and argue that glaring inconsistencies here show that we are hugely ambivalent about the value of children. I will also argue that our current process places GPs in an intolerable, invidious position. Our law's failure to specify what the grounds for legal abortion actually are makes it virtually impossible for GPs to act according to conscience without potentially being (wrongly) accused of inappropriately imposing their own morality upon patients. Our doctors are being deeply wronged by the current system.

This process is deeply flawed; our doctors are being deeply wronged.

In Chapter Four I conclude by arguing that we need to tell ourselves the truth about our practice of abortion, and offering some suggestions for re-enlivening the debate about it.

2 Abortion On Demand?

What is the actual process by which a pregnant woman can, for whatever reason, have an abortion performed?

This must be understood for us to see the *shape* of the ethical issues I am pursuing. The morality of abortion itself is often discussed. However, the morality of the way in which a decision is actually reached in each case—and therefore the ethical shape of the question for a woman deciding whether to carry her child or not, and for the doctor whose agreement is needed if she is to have an abortion—has been rather neglected.

According to The Abortion Act 1967, as amended in the Human Fertilization and Embryology Act 1990, the legal requirement for an elective abortion to proceed is for two doctors to sign form HSA 1, certifying that one or more of five listed criteria for permitting abortion apply. The form reads:

We [the two signatory doctors] hereby certify that we are of the opinion, formed in good faith, that in the case of [name]:

A the continuance of the pregnancy would involve risk to the life of the pregnant woman greater than if the pregnancy were terminated

B the termination is necessary to prevent grave permanent injury to the physical or mental health of the pregnant woman

C the pregnancy has NOT exceeded its 24th week and the continuance of the pregnancy would involve risk, greater than if the pregnancy were terminated, of injury to the physical or mental health of the pregnant woman

D the pregnancy has NOT exceeded its 24th week and the continuance of the pregnancy would involve risk, greater than if the pregnancy were terminated, of injury to the physical or mental health of any existing child(ren) of the family of the pregnant woman

E there is a substantial risk that if the child were born it would suffer from such physical or mental abnormalities as to be seriously handicapped.

There are further legal categories F and G, on a second certificate, allowing for abortion to save the life of the mother or save her from grave harm. Obviously, these do not appear on the form for elective abortion.

The normal procedure is for a pregnant woman wanting to seek an abortion or discuss her situation to visit her GP.[8] For an abortion to proceed, the GP must sign the form, indicating which (one or more) of criteria A–E are satisfied, and refer the woman to clinic; the second signatory on the form will be a doctor at the clinic where the abortion is performed. If the GP signs, this second signature is almost invariably given. While the Act specified *two* doctors' signatures to offer some security that a considered medical judgment was being made, in practice the second is really a formality.

If the GP does not sign, he or she may yet refer the patient to clinic, where the woman will be seen by two doctors, both of whom must sign the form; the procurement of two signatures still follows almost invariably in this case.

Should a GP refuse to sign or refer,[9] the pregnant woman may well go to another partner in the practice or even to another GP, or to a private clinic.[10] Obviously, this places GPs who in conscience will not sign (except in rare limit cases) in a very difficult position. If they normally do not sign forms, should they declare this in every consultation as soon as it becomes clear that a woman may be considering an abortion? One could argue that they should, for completing the consultation only to then declare that they normally do not sign raises questions about patient care—why continue such a consultation, if the result will be only to pass the patient on to a colleague, subjecting the pregnant woman to the painful business of disclosing and explaining her situation again to another health professional? However, if for these reasons GPs who are basically against abortion choose not to see patients who may ultimately seek abortion, this is hardly helpful to women unsure about what to do and genuinely seeking counsel. Such patients are then effectively denied access to GPs whose perspective they might value in reaching a decision, or who might helpfully refer them to a Pregnancy Crisis Centre. Ironically, a pro-life stance would then result in that GP being unavailable to women who might yet choose to keep their child, given the full range of advice and opinion. Therefore, Christian GPs often decide to participate in the process, hoping to do some good rather than none, albeit risking considerable ambiguity as they do so.

Christian GPs often decide to participate in the process, hoping to do some good rather than none

GPs are also aware that by not signing forms they will continually be passing patients on to colleagues. The increase in overall work-load and routine channelling of abortion requests to colleagues who are often equally uneasy about such consultations easily creates tensions within the practice.

This process, then, places Christian GPs (and others opposed to abortion) in an acutely uncomfortable position. Wanting to be genuinely helpful to their patients, reluctant to off-load abortion work onto colleagues, aspiring to act ethically without inappropriately imposing their own morality, many GPs dread abortion consultations. They feel there is no good method of handling requests, which allows them to balance their ethics with good patient care, especially given the reality that many women arrive determined to procure an abortion.

What the Criteria Mean

To fully appreciate the position GPs are placed in we must understand what constitutes a legal abortion in England and Wales by examining the criteria from form HSA 1.[11]

Clauses A and B (and F and G) refer to a strictly medical judgment about the health of the pregnant woman; in rare cases, a pregnancy can clearly, directly threaten her life or health. In such cases no GP would refuse to sign, knowingly risking a mother's life in order possibly to give life to a child. However, clauses A or B are very rarely used. In 1999, only 103 abortions—0.06% of a total 173,701[12]—were performed under Clause A (alone or in conjunction with other clauses) or in emergency (F and G). Under Clause B (alone, or in conjunction with C or D), 1,836 (1.06%) were permitted.

Clause E allows abortion on the grounds of substantial risk of the child being seriously handicapped. This raises many questions. What constitutes 'serious' handicap? Abnormalities that mean a child has a low life-expectancy? Or will suffer great pain without hope of long life? Spinabifida? Down's syndrome? Even if we could agree on a definition of 'seriously handicapped' (none is given), we have to ask why we presume that the handicapped have less right to life and less of a claim upon the welcome of their parents and society as a whole than others. Why are they less valuable than other children? Of course, there is no intrinsic reason why this should be so at all; it is the interests of, responsibilities of, and pressures upon *parents* that are at issue here.

We have to ask why we presume that the handicapped have less right to life

This devaluation of life because of handicap in the unborn is hugely, staggeringly at odds with our political and social morality with respect to handicapped members of society. Just try to argue that handicapped people should have fewer rights or are less valuable than other people *because* of their handicap, and legal as well as moral wrath will rapidly (and rightly) follow. However, this defence of the disabled is not extended to the unborn. To receive the gradually improving rights of the disabled you have to get yourself born, and Clause E offers sufficient grounds to prevent just that.

So I do not concede that this criterion is normally morally acceptable. However, even if we allow that there may be a reasonable debate over certain cases here, we are still talking about a small minority of abortions. In 1999 only 1,813 abortions (1.04%) were carried out under Clause E (alone, or with C or D).

The vast majority, almost 98%, of abortions in England and Wales are carried out under Clauses C and D, and here the issues I am concerned with arise. These clauses allow for abortion before 24 weeks of pregnancy if 'the continuance of the pregnancy would involve risk, greater than if the pregnancy were terminated, of injury' either 'to the physical or mental health of the pregnant woman' (C) or 'to the physical or mental health of any existing child(ren) of the family of the pregnant woman' (D).

Ostensibly medical criteria are routinely interpreted to permit abortion on social grounds

Most abortions are authorized under Clause C alone: 159,444 (91.79%) in 1999; a further 10,553 (6.05%) were accepted under Clause D (alone or with C). I pursue some ethical implications of the use of these clauses, which were introduced in the 1990 amendment, in the next chapter. In preparation for that, let us make four observations about these Clauses.

Clauses C and D

First, these two clauses speak of *health risks*. Abortion is apparently being authorized because continuing the pregnancy poses a quantifiable *health* risk to the mother or existing children. But what injury or risks do these criteria actually refer to? *No definition of what constitutes injury to the physical or mental health of either the woman or her children is offered* (and it cannot be the direct threat already specified in Clauses A and B); this is left entirely to the interpretation of the signatory doctors, the first of whom is usually the GP. Therefore, the vast majority of abortions are permitted according to criteria that are not regulated by any professionally or publicly agreed interpretation whatsoever.

Secondly, while these grounds are ostensibly medical, *they can be and are routinely interpreted to permit abortion on social grounds*. Clauses A and B already cover immediate and clear medical risks of potential harm to the mother, and no strictly medical definition is given of the risk or harm envisaged by C and D. The 1990 Act stated that 'in determining whether the continuance of the pregnancy would involve such risk of injury to health…account may be taken of the pregnant woman's actual or reasonably foreseeable environment.'[13] These criteria can therefore be used to authorize abortions for reasons that are basically social, concerning the relative ability of a woman to care for a child, or simply her desire to do so as opposed to pursuing other goals in life. Undefined mental health risks to a woman or her children are broad categories indeed; any woman preferring an abortion to the obvious stress of bearing and raising a child *can* be interpreted as at risk of mental harm by continuing her pregnancy. The 1994 Rawlinson (Private Commission of Inquiry) Report, 'The Physical and Psycho-Social Effects of Abortion on Women,' found that 45% of women sought abortion because of partner pressure or unstable relationship; for 26% financial circumstances were important; for 15% family, study or career considerations were highly relevant.[14] Under cover of an ostensibly medical judgment, many abortions are performed for social reasons.

The life of the unbor. is not weighed as a benefit against poter tial harm to the motI

Consequently, these two clauses provide the effective basis for abortion upon request on social grounds. A woman's circumstances may be agonizingly difficult, or it may be entirely possible for her to proceed with the pregnancy, just undesired; in either case, and at all stations between, Clauses C and D will often be accepted as relevant.

Thirdly, *the value of the unborn child is irrelevant:* the life of the unborn is not weighed as a benefit against potential harm to the mother in these clauses. For any woman who wants her child, the obvious discomfort, sickness and (small) actual risk in pregnancy are perfectly acceptable when held in balance against the huge value of a child. However, if the unborn child has no accepted value or claim upon the welcome of the parents unless they confer it, then *any* perceived risk to the mother becomes acceptable grounds for abortion. Every pregnancy involves *some* level of change, sickness and risk; hence, Clause C can be interpreted to mean that *any* pregnancy of itself, by default, entails reasonable grounds for its own termination. This cannot be what the 1967 Act intended.

In all other branches of medicine we are cautious about offering treatments if we are unsure about possible serious side-effects

Fourthly, there is *no recognition of possible risks to a woman in having an abortion*. This area is heavily disputed. The debate about 'Post Abortion Syndrome'

(PAS) and serious emotional damage from abortion is raging,[15] and links between abortion and breast cancer, chlamydial infection and infertility are also under investigation. However, while a significant (albeit disputed) number of those who have abortions undergo substantial guilt and grief, our process neither recognizes this risk nor balances it against the 'risk' of continuing the pregnancy. If risk to the mother is really the issue, there should be a complex calculation of alternative risks, with the possibility of post-abortion trauma assessed seriously. We cannot know the *exact* risks of having an abortion; however, in all other branches of medicine we are cautious about offering treatments if we are unsure about possible serious side-effects.

Putting it Together

To sum up: Clauses C and D can be applied on grounds that are not strictly medical, in terms of quantifiable risk (Clause B would be used here), but basically social, concerning the perceived stress of having a child. This effectively provides abortion upon request for those who do not want the child they are carrying, as long as the GP, gynaecologist(s) or private clinic doctors concerned are ready to interpret the Clauses in this way.[16] I am not suggesting that social grounds are necessarily insignificant. Some women will be facing major issues of stress, financial constraint and lack of support; the desperation of many is real. Still, it is important to be clear: we can and do practise abortion upon demand for social reasons, although the decision is made on ostensibly medical grounds. It seems most unlikely that supporters of the 1967 Act intended this. Certainly, pro-abortionists now complain that our legislation makes it possible for some doctors to interpret the legislation 'restrictively' and refuse to sign forms on social grounds; others would argue that such a 'restrictive' medical interpretation is appropriate, and the weakness is rather that an unintended social interpretation became possible after 1990. What we know is that 98% of abortions are permitted on the unspecified, vague grounds possible under Clauses C and D.

98% of abortions are permitted on the unspecified, vague grounds possible under Clauses C and D

This process raises many ethical questions. We should ask what beliefs and values it is encouraging our society to hold about pregnancy and the worth of children, and what it is demanding of and doing to our GPs. This is our task in Chapter Three.

3 What We Are Telling Ourselves

In Huxley's Brave New World *social conditioning was achieved partly through the repetition of the chosen values and beliefs of the World State during the sleep of children.*

We do not practise hypnopaedia, but we do tell ourselves a certain tale about the unborn around 174,000 times a year through abortion. What is that story, and what values is it conditioning us with? Who do we become if we believe it? Our current abortion process has a number of ethical implications; I will discuss five areas in this chapter.

1. Pregnancy as Illness

Some friends of mine once took a walking holiday together, one in an advanced stage of pregnancy. In the up-hill banter there was much teasing about her slack pace; when this wore thin she responded, 'It's not an illness, you know.' However, the criteria by which most pregnancies are terminated mean that we are coming to treat pregnancy, functionally, as precisely that: an illness for which there is a cure. The undefined risk of injury in pregnancy spoken of in Clauses C and D opens the door to viewing pregnancy in itself as a negative, harmful state, if we choose to do so.

The prospect of receiving a child always carries some anxiety. There is often an understandable sense of unreadiness for parenthood, and some fear about changes that will come (to lifestyle, sleep, other relationships, work, and so on). This is, however, natural and appropriate. What would the gift of a new life be worth, if not tinged with awe about who this child will be, what her arrival will mean for her parents, and whether they will be equal to the task of nurturing a child? Pregnancy itself brings some inherent disruption and usually sickness too, early on; later it brings discomfort, and finally pain in child-birth. This is what happens; it goes with the territory, in bringing new people into the world. Some pregnancies are more complicated, and a small number are dangerous to the mother in ways that cannot usually be predicted in advance.

Clearly, every pregnancy entails some risk and therefore a 'greater' risk of injury than would be the case if the woman had not become pregnant. This level of risk is obvious, and has always been regarded as relatively insignificant when weighed against the value of the gift being received through pregnancy. However, Clauses C and D allow us to focus entirely upon the 'risk' pregnancy brings, ruling out any counterbalancing sense of the value of the unborn. Clause C allows us to redescribe pregnancy purely in terms of threat to the mother. Remember that we are not talking about serious risk to the mother's life or health here—Clauses A, B, F and G cover these possibilities—but harm as perceived by the mother and doctor.

We allow pregnancy to be selectively redefined as an affliction, a sexually-transmitted disease

My simple point is that without any definition of injury or risk to govern this, we allow pregnancy in itself, with the usual risks inherent in the miracle of child-bearing, to be selectively redefined as an affliction, a malady, a sexually-transmitted disease. Society should ask whether it wishes to accept this account of pregnancy. Certainly, from a Christian point of view, it is tragic. The condition from which women sought deliverance in Scripture was barrenness, not pregnancy, and children are viewed biblically as a blessing from God.

There is nothing inherently different about the pregnancies that are terminated under Clauses C and D from those which are continued. However, the former (98% of terminated pregnancies) are redefined as illness presenting unacceptable risk, according to the mother's prediction about the impact upon her or her other children of bearing a child.

Furthermore, our process tells us as a society that pregnancy is an illness for which there is a cure. It is not known how effective this cure really is; post-abortion injury is disputed. Still, while the incidence of serious grief and ongoing regret is debated, some level of trauma is clearly not rare. Certainly, if abortion is seen to offer complete cure—a return to the pre-pregnancy state of the woman—this is a delusion. For abortion offers not a return to the situation prior to pregnancy, but simply a different post-pregnancy future than that in which there is a child. Reality is affected,

Abortion offers not a return to the pre-pregnancy state, but simply a different post-pregnancy future

but not *reversed*; rather, it now includes the momentous decision in a woman's personal history of ending a life that would otherwise have continued as her child.

Re-imagining unwanted pregnancy as curable illness is a way of further diminishing responsibility for becoming pregnant. Contracting a disease matters much less if there is a cure. (If AIDs could be cured, safer sex would be even harder to promote.) Furthermore, the message that we can be cured of pregnancy and all its inconvenience is hugely welcome to a society in which individual freedom, and being able to 'continue with my life,' is seen as an almost indubitable good. Many GPs report that most women who have an abortion still believe it to be 'wrong'; this is confirmed by recent American research in which *pro-choice* women saw abortion unambiguously as killing.[17] So why do people convinced that they are about to do something wrong still proceed? Anecdotally, many believe they have 'no choice.' Plainly, most *do* have choices, but the other options (going to term and either keeping a child or offering him or her for adoption) are extremely *hard* choices.

Pregnancy does not need curing; it needs courage, and huge support, for a good course to be chosen

By defining abortion as a curable malady we both mask women's widely shared sense that this is wrong, and offer the illusion of a path back to their pre-pregnant life.

'The terrible miscalculation of young women is that abortion can make them "unpregnant," that it will restore them to who they were before their crisis. But a woman is never the same once she is pregnant, whether the child is kept, adopted, or killed. Abortion may be a kind of resolution; it is not the one the woman most deeply longs for, nor will it even preserve her sense of self.'[18]

However, our process misleadingly teaches that pregnancy is a morally neutral and entirely reversible state, giving a person their pre-pregnancy life back. So my first criticism of our abortion process is that it is allowing us to treat unwanted pregnancy as curable illness, which is deceptive and damaging. Pregnancy does not need curing; it needs courage, and huge support, for a good course to be chosen.

2. The (De)Valuation of Children

I have argued that Clauses C and D can be and are interpreted to mean that in any situation where a woman decides a birth will make life more difficult for her or her children, she effectively has a case for abortion. The rather obvious recognition that children change us and our lives has become sufficient grounds to justify abortion. Our decision-making process has become wholly unsuited to its consequence, the grave moral act which it allows. This system means that the value of each foetus can be defined strictly according to its mother's own personal acceptance or rejection. In this voluntaristic approach, no sense of the unborn child's value or (better) claim upon our welcome intrudes at all. Given this, my next question concerns what we are telling ourselves as a society as we repeat and internalize the message that value is only *conferred* upon children by choice of others.

By allowing value to be conferred or withheld in this way we diminish the value of *all* children. If an unborn child is not valued because she is unique, or has undeniable human worth, or inalienable human rights, or because welcoming our children is simply what we *do* as humans, let alone because she is created in the image of God, then a child who is born has value merely because in her particular case she was wanted by her parent(s). It is perfectly possible that she could *not* have been wanted; annually, around 174,000 (20% of unborn children) are not. Just like winning the National Lottery—except at much shorter odds in this lottery—'it could be you,' or any child, aborted. Now, if we can decide some are of no worth because we do *not* want them, what real value can we confer on those we decide

This is public, social policy, and we are all surely affected by the story we are telling ourselves

we *do* want?[19] Nothing intrinsic, or to do with who they are as human, or as children (ours or God's). If a mother told her growing child that, actually, she had *nearly* chosen to have him aborted, we would correctly see that as intolerable, abusive, cruel behaviour. Yet this is the message that we increasingly give to all the children of our society, and this must be (mis-)shaping us.

This is fundamentally opposed to a Christian vision of the dignity and value of life as given by God. *We* do not choose how valuable people are; God does, and we are called to receive and nurture people, particularly those who are weakest and most need protection, whether infants, the marginalized, the refugee or even the enemy. Our abortion process offers a contrary ethic, telling us we have the right to decide who lives. This process is a legal matter, and indeed part of *health* care within a national *health* service, implemented through the agency of our doctors. This is public, social policy, and we are all surely affected by the story we are telling ourselves.

We value wanted conceived infants more than unwanted conceived children

Significantly, other valuations of pregnancy in our society contradict this story. Most mothers receive their child with joy. Some people are desperate, and willing to go to great lengths and expense, to have children. Compare the choice to abort a conceived child with the determination of others to become pregnant, struggling through several tests and rounds of IVF treatment. Totally incompatible valuations of unborn children coexist within our society, our health service and even within the same hospital ward. Hence, hospital chaplains often receive requests from women who have miscarried for funeral services for their lost 'child.' These foetuses— often young enough to be aborted legally if the parent(s) felt differently about receiving them—are treated by their parents and hospital staff as *children*, and grieved for as such. In January 2002 a media scandal broke over a hospital mortuary losing the body of 'James Kelly'; no doubt was cast on whether James mattered, or should have been treated with dignity, or was a child, or about the grief his parents suffered. James Kelly died at 22 weeks, within the time when he could legally have been aborted.

So our society is becoming one where we value a child if we want it, and value it highly enough (economically) in expensive IVF treatment such that other significant possible medical goods are sacrificed. Yet we place that value only on wanted children. Indeed, we value—economically and in other ways—the *unconceived* infants of parents who want children more than the *conceived* children of those who do not. We allocate some medical resources to the destruction of foetuses for some parents, even as we allocate far greater medical resources to their creation for others. We advise mothers of unborn children about alcohol, diet and exercise in the interests of the 'health' of their unborn 'child' (our language); their well-being is considered important because they are wanted. Research apparently shows the value of playing babies in the womb soothing music, either to make them musical, soothed, or both, and some act on this advice too. But for unborn children who are in themselves medically just as viable, only not wanted, considerations of alcohol units, unpasteurized eggs and cheese and *in utero* helpings of Mozart are irrelevant, because their well-being is irrelevant; they will be removed. We must ask if the valuation placed upon the unborn by their mothers is sufficient grounds for their different treatment—to one, all possible protection, even from the potential assault of camembert; to the other, termination.

When is a baby not a baby? When you do not want it

In one episode of *Friends*, in advance of the implantation of IVF embryos, Phoebe talks to them in the dish. It is humorous, but revealing. In the very language we use in our society and health-care services, when is a baby—in the womb—a baby? When you want it. When is a baby not a baby? When you do not want it. Can we live with that set of scales? And what are we becoming if we do?

3. The Privatisation of Moral Choice

That the valuation of a child's life should effectively be determined with absolute finality by an individual, under the vague terms of Clause C, should worry us. The slogan of the National Abortion Campaign (NAC) is, 'Our bodies, our lives, our right to decide.' Clause C's current application gives the NAC little to complain about. However, unless it really is true that there is 'no such thing as society,' the whole business of conceiving and bearing children is *not* a wholly private matter, and decisions about the treatment of the unborn should not be treated as wholly private either.

st like the life of e child itself, the alth of society is a consideration

I believe that our slogan should be something like, 'Our relationships, our responsibilities, our welcome of children.' However, there is no space on HSA 1 to indicate that in the opinion of the doctors the termination of the pregnancy would involve risk, greater than if the pregnancy were continued, of injury to the health of *society*. Just like the life of the child itself, that is simply not a consideration. This is a real problem, unless we genuinely believe that human worth is to be determined privately.

It is not just wider society that is being excluded from decisions affecting it here; the privatisation of choice has effects nearer home too. In our abortion procedure (particularly under Clause C), it is solely the woman's predicted welfare and her decision that counts. This militates against including the father in discussion; his views about the pregnancy are not legally relevant. While many fathers may sadly not wish to be involved, this is part of the *problem*, not something to be accepted or encouraged procedurally. Part of our malaise is the irresponsibility of men and couples in conceiving unwanted children, so bringing the father into the process and sharing the responsibility is an important goal.[20] Our system, however, reinforces very negative patterns of paternal irresponsibility. If the hard but good path of finding support to keep a child is to be found, then the pregnancy and future childcare need to be shared by drawing in, wherever possible, the father, his family, the mother's family, and friends. Instead, by our system we exclude all other parties even from consultation by making this purely an issue of a woman's choices and rights.

The more private pregnancy is made, the less possible is seems to bear a child

The more private pregnancy is made, the less possible it seems to bear a child. Our system privatises the decision-making, isolating it from any positive moral framework or possible community. Is the abortion of healthy foetuses a private matter, or an issue of society's attitude to, treatment of and welcome of human life? Is receiving a child the responsibility of an isolated, frightened woman, or of a couple, families, and communities? From a Christian point of view, we are systematically getting the answer to these questions wrong at the moment.

4. The Commodification of Children

Our ability simply to decide whether we do or do not want a child corresponds with a trend to make the having of children a lifestyle issue. We face a growing commodification of children, in which we implicitly treat them as possessions rather than persons, objects of our choice rather than subjects who are given life and entrusted to us only by the grace of God. Assisted reproduction cannot but help create a sense in which children are now being made at our choice; furthermore, we will be tempted to feel that 'if we make a child, we determine its meaning and use.'[21] This is not to say that assisted reproduction is wrong, but to recognize an attendant moral danger.

Other pressures towards commodifying children are yet more obvious. Surrogacy encourages a sense that we can always get children if we really want them. In 2001 scandals broke over internet adoption agencies effectively selling babies—sometimes twice! And a Scottish couple who had four sons challenged British laws forbidding gender selection; having tragically lost their daughter, they fought for the right to conceive (only) a girl. If we would be unwilling to receive a child that God gives us, whether due to handicap or (in this case) a predetermination of desired gender, we must ask why we have children at all. In a Christian framework, it is not meant to be for our benefit, and certainly not to our requirements; we receive children as a gift to care for, nurture, and share the love of God with. But in our society the pressure to turn everything into a matter of consumer choice now touches even children. If we are basically free to reject some conceived children altogether, we will find ourselves left with little argument against the choosing of gender and genetic characteristics in planned conceptions.

Having a child is no longer necessarily seen as placing a responsibility on us

Having a child is increasingly spoken of as a *right*; at the same time, having actually conceived a child is no longer necessarily seen as placing a *responsibility* on us. We are already well along the path of choosing, individually, what we want, and—given our abortion process—it will be very hard to stop this process leading to other morally undesirable consequences.

5. The (Ab)Use of Doctors and the Violence of the System

I have argued that up to 98% of abortions are made by a woman's decision on basically social rather than strictly medical grounds. However, it is doctors who sign the form, and the use of medical professionals to authorize abortions on essentially social grounds is highly questionable and in many ways repugnant.

Most Christian (and many other) GPs loathe abortion consultations. Dedicated professionally to working for the health of their patients, and using their skill and energy to enhance and save life, in these cases they are instead placed under pressure to authorize decisions to end life. The value of the unborn child is something the process excludes from the decision; doctors who presume to suggest the life of the foetus is an ethical consideration sometimes face condemnation. This makes GPs vulnerable to the accusation of imposing *their* morality upon a patient, while the assumption that a pro-abortion morality is somehow neutral and uncontroversial is widespread.

The absence of any definition of harm in Clauses C and D makes it virtually impossible for GPs to refuse to sign without potentially being accused of this inappropriate intrusion of their ethics upon their 'medical' decision. Furthermore, doctors are not only expected to suspend their morality, but to adopt *conflicting* moralities depending upon the choices of different mothers. It is assumed that they and other health professionals will alternately give good antenatal care to wanted 'babies' (our language), then adopt a completely different approach to unwanted foetuses. GPs are coerced into treating pregnancy as a negative medical condition and a foetus as of little or no inherent worth, as and when the patient so determines.[22] We ask our doctors not only to suspend their own morality, but also to operate according to the contradictory moral valuations of unborn children brought to them by different people. We should, in the interests of truth, honesty, and the health of all concerned, have a different process.

Doctors are effectively being used through this process as society's agents in abortion

Doctors are effectively being used through this process as society's agents in abortion. To deal with 175,000 unwanted children per annum, and give a semblance of respectability to their removal, we have two doctors sign the form.

The 1967 Act allows doctors to refuse to sign forms as a matter of conscience. However, I indicated in Chapter Two why this may cause tension within a practice and lead to real questions about patient care, and why pro-life GPs often remain involved in abortion consultations as the lesser of two evils. In actual practice, many Christian GPs find no good way to handle these dilemmas and end up being used as part of a system in which social abortion on demand is basically available but dressed up as medically acceptable.

The current abortion process is therefore violent towards our GPs. We use those trained to promote health to end healthy lives. Valid concerns are always expressed about what trust patients could possibly extend to GPs if we ever permit euthanasia and involve doctors in it. However, we already use GPs to authorize the rejection and removal of healthy but unborn children; this too is contrary to their calling and to the role we should wish to see them play in our society. We place them in a position where it seems impossible to act according to conscience. This system is violent towards our doctors whom we are abusing and harming.

The system is also violent towards women, in that it excludes considerations of the possible physical, mental and emotional damage women may bring upon themselves.[23] Who is truly on the side of women here? The pro-choice lobby? Anyone claiming to have women's interests truly at heart must be willing to investigate honestly the damage that abortion may do to women. It is extremely difficult for GPs to enter this territory, but the system could demand that counsellors with experience of helping women with post-abortion trauma should be seen as part of their decision-making process. Furthermore, in privatising the decision about abortion we do not necessarily increase choice for women. We isolate them from their family, partners and community, and often *limit* choice by so doing. This is not good for women either.

Who is truly c the side of women here?

I also suggest that our system is injurious to a third group, men, both in excluding them and colluding with their own refusal to accept co-responsibility. We are not helping men to learn a better way, because the 'illness' that is pregnancy can be 'cured' so easily.

The process is violent towards those children born only because they happened to be wanted

Fourthly, the process is violent towards society, because it is teaching us that we do not have responsibility towards one another and that there is no intrinsic value to human life. Finally, of course, it is violent towards children, especially to those not born because they were not wanted, but also to those born only because they happened to be wanted.

There has to be a better way forward than this. In the concluding chapter I offer some suggestions for a Christian response to this issue and offer some modest suggestions for working towards change.

Telling the Truth and Welcoming Children

4

Through our abortion process we are telling ourselves a certain story about pregnancy, children, life and our right to choose.
Unpacking and examining the beliefs and values wrapped up in this process is important. We need to tell the truth about who we are, or are becoming. Beyond that, from our Christian faith, can we offer a vision of pregnancy and of receiving children that challenges the account our current abortion system encourages? This is the task of this final chapter.

Telling the Truth About Ourselves

This booklet does not offer a full theological or biblical pro-life argument. It is primarily an appeal, in a Christian voice, that we should tell the truth about our current abortion process and what it is making of us. Who are we?

We are currently a society where children are increasingly welcomed or rejected according to a person's will, at that particular moment in time, to have a child or not. I acknowledge that this willingness may be affected by hugely complicated factors. Nevertheless, it remains the case that we are the kind of people who cannot be relied upon to welcome our own children: 20% of the time we reject them, and about a third of all women will reject a child at some point.[24]

About a third of all women will reject a child at some point

We are people who proceed with abortion in spite of a very high valuation of the unborn in other circumstances, and a widely shared view even among women who have abortions that it is wrong. We do not even let the ethical debate have any formal place in the practical decision-making process.

We are also people who make our doctors, especially our 'family' doctors, inappropriately bear the pain and confusion of dealing with abortion requests. We use them to do our work in a duplicitous way. As things stand, we are (ab)using our health professionals to damage the health of women, children and society, effectively making them act contrary to profession and conscience, but telling ourselves they are making decisions in the best medical interests of women and other children. At best we do not know that; at worst, it is a systematic and very useful deception.

We are not telling the truth. We say we are performing abortions in the interests of people's health, but this is at best only partly true. We certainly do not ensure that women hear about the possible long-term emotional risks in having an abortion; even if we cannot accurately assess risk here, telling the truth would demand that we say 'we do not know how risky this is' to those considering an abortion. We give an impression of *necessity* (if it is on health grounds, and the doctor agreed, it must have been right…) to *chosen* paths, so again we are misleading ourselves. This untruth is perpetuated at the expense of doctors, women and the unborn.

Telling the Truth About God: Life As Gift

What Christian vision might inspire a new resistance to the voluntarism of our society about which unborn children may live? Can our faith offer a positive vision that challenges abortion on demand? I concur with those who say that abortion is wrong simply because life is God's gift, and not ours to take.

We understand that the love and care of good parents communicates to the child the prior, ultimate love and valuation of that child by God, as Father and Creator. Karl Barth argued that the analogy of God as Father is only superficially understood if we think that through observing good parents we see what God is like; more fundamentally, he said, it is the love of God the Father which teaches us what good parenting is. While some object that in human terms analogies cannot work like that, Barth's theological point is vital—the love of God is prior to human love, and gives it its being. Similarly, the parenthood of God is prior to ours, and our loving, unconditional parenthood communicates God's. The value of every child is fundamentally as a child of God, and it is this which is communicated through good human parenting.

Life as God's gift is being mutated into life as our choice

Our society is currently practising and preaching a denial of this, as through our abortion process we arrogate to ourselves the right to decide which of the unborn are to be valued enough—against all the difficulties and challenges their being will bring—to be allowed to *be*. Once we allow ourselves to choose that some who are perfectly viable medically should not live, without their claim upon us even being considered, we devalue all. Life as (God's) gift is being mutated into life as our choice. Once this shift has been made, even when we say 'yes' to a life, our valuation remains only conditional, and when we say 'no' we are being violent. We are shaping society according to the belief that we can decide who lives, and that diminishes the value of all hugely.

22

We are called instead to welcome children, very simply, as God-given gifts, and to see parenthood not as a burden, but as a trust and a calling. Unborn children perhaps have a 'right to life,' though I am wary of some of our 'rights' language. They certainly have a claim upon our welcome and hospitality, because they are loved by God and he requires that we extend his love to them by welcoming, nurturing and loving them.[25] Our mandate here is not only the command to participate in God's creation by multiplying, nor only the prohibition of killing in the Decalogue, nor only the strong scriptural theme of welcoming and supporting the weak, but also Jesus' command to love. We are called upon to love as Christ loved us, which of course is not a love without suffering or cost.

We are called upon to love as Christ loved us, which of course is not a love without suffering or cost

This means being willing to parent *and to support parents* not because it is to our benefit, but because it benefits others, especially children who we might otherwise reject, were it not for this command to love them instead.

To witness to this belief, we need to object strenuously to the current (de)valuation, commodification and conditional approval of children which our abortion law allows and encourages. Christian witness demands this, and we must not leave it only to our doctors to make this stand. They are being abused enough already.

Making the Truth Tell: Some Practical Measures?

Caught between a vision of life as gift and a society increasingly refusing the gift or making it conditional, at this depressing stage in the struggle over abortion, what can we do?

First, we should be *trying to re-enliven the debate not just about abortion in itself but about British law and 'medical' practice*. We are almost tired of hearing anti-abortion arguments, partly because most evangelical and Catholic Christians are convinced they are right anyway! But the wider debate is not lively. I suggest that, tactically, we might focus a renewed challenge specifically on the current process by demanding clarification of what the criteria in Clauses C and D actually *mean*. We should argue that these are masking social abortion on demand, and stimulate a debate about whether that is acceptable.

Secondly, *we should be pressing for a process that is fitting for the weight of the act it allows*. In Britain, we look at the policy on gun control in the United States, and are utterly bemused. For such a weighty, potentially grave matter as owning a firearm, we feel their process for obtaining one (buying one over a

23

counter) is wholly insufficient. However, the same applies to the process by which one can obtain an abortion in England and Wales. One would hope that for a decision of such importance as abortion we would have a process that would allow, even demand, that all possible options are considered, with the mother given counsel about the possible consequences of each course of action and about the different moral views concerning this act. There should be an appropriately serious process for such a weighty decision. Our current system purports to be significant (two whole signatures, both from qualified doctors) but this has become very deceptive, masking the reality of what is often happening.

Thirdly, as part of such a genuinely serious approach, we need to *reintroduce the claim of the unborn child into the process*, in some realistic way. We should pursue the issue of the value and status of the life of the unborn, not least by challenging our society to address its own currently irreconcilable views of the status of the unborn and the value of pregnancy. People should feel acutely uncomfortable over the discrepancies in our language about and treatment of the unborn in, on the one hand, abortion and, on the other, assisted reproduction, good ante-natal care and grief over miscarriage. Our contradictions are evidenced in both popular perception and medical practice. We are living by incompatible stories, and we can and should use this to demonstrate that we are deceiving ourselves about abortion.

> *People should feel acutely uncomfortable over the discrepancies in our language about the unborn*

Fourthly, we need to *encourage the hard but good path of women bearing their children*. The church needs to find ways of leading in this, by welcoming and befriending pregnant women who are anxious about continuing their pregnancy, and supporting them in their parenting. The many committed Christians who are involved in counselling and pregnancy crisis services have a prophetic voice that needs to be heard more by Christians, and to guide the churches. Our seemingly simplistic belief in life as God's gift will be more powerfully witnessed to if we put more of our God-given energy into helping women receive their gift of a child, in practical ways. To take this seriously could change us. For Christians to genuinely welcome, befriend and support pregnant women in crisis, putting our money and energy where our pro-life mouths are, would probably do more than anything else to make a difference. Finding ways to support women struggling to choose to keep their babies is probably the most loving and practical thing we can do.

If we were willing to offer such support, my fifth suggestion would be that we need to *encourage the hard but good path for some of carrying their children and offering them for adoption.* If it is the case that:

(a) there are many people who genuinely wish to parent but cannot conceive, and there is a great shortage of babies available for adoption;

(b) many women after abortion do suffer considerable ongoing distress;

(c) as most people still believe, abortion is a bad thing

then can we support women enough to carry their child to full term, so that someone else willing and able to raise that child may do so? Such encouragement will need more than words: it will need resourcing, demanding government support for agencies willing to support pregnant women in this situation.

Sixth, we can *argue that it is appropriate for GPs to refer women to Pregnancy Crisis Centres* as an acceptable and normal part of the process. There is a lurking sense that only effectively pro-choice advice is neutral or unbiased. On the contrary, women *should* have the opportunity of advice and support from a pro-life agency as part of the process of deciding what to do about their pregnancy.

There is a lurking sense that only effectively pro-choice advice is neutral or unbiased

Conclusion

Such steps might help move us towards becoming a society that welcomes its children, and takes responsibility for those we conceive. We are a long way from such a land, and the journey towards it looks highly problematic. A Christian vision of life as gift and its consequences may seem so far from the grim reality of our abortion process that there is no real connection. It is our task as Christians to hold out an alternative, disruptive vision. We need also to find practical ways, within a plural and post-Christian society, of challenging the current process, so that we move nearer to becoming a people who welcome all our children, not just 80% of them. If we could begin by telling the truth, that would help.

Notes

1   See Sian Kerslake, 'Abortion,' in M D Beer (ed), *Christian Choices in Health Care* (Leicester: IVP, 1995) pp 163-176.

2   See O O'Donovan, *The Christian and the Unborn Child* (Grove Ethics booklet E 1); G Meilaender, *Bioethics for Christians* (Grand Rapids: Eerdmans, 1996), pp 26-38; R B Hays, *The Moral Vision of the New Testament* (Edinburgh: T&T Clark, 1997) pp 444-461.

3   I recognize that all terms in this area—abortion, killing, unborn child—are controversial. The words themselves are significant, for different terms mean different things. Hence, I will not normally refer to 'termination' of pregnancy, for that is not a synonym for 'abortion' of a child. On using the right language as Christians, see S Hauerwas, 'Abortion—Theologically Understood' in P Stallsworth (ed), *The Church and Abortion* (Nashville: Abingdon Press, 1993), pp 52-54.

4   See statistics on the number of abortions performed under different criteria in Chapter 2.

5   E Burton and A Fergusson, *Christian Medical Fellowship Member's Attitudes to Abortion: A Survey of Reported Views and Practice* (London: CMF, 1996) pp 9, 15-19.

6   'There are apparent discrepancies between belief and behaviour,' *ibid*, p 19.

7   See Nanas Callander, 'Dealing in the GP Surgery with a Request for Termination of Pregnancy,' *Journal of the Christian Medical Fellowship*, January 1996, pp 11-14.

8   A few Primary Care Groups now use nurse-led clinics for initial consultation; however, the majority of decisions about abortion begin procedurally with a visit to the GP.

9   A doctor would refuse to sign if he or she did not see any of the criteria on the form applying, or if he or she exercises the legal right of conscience of all doctors to refuse to participate in abortion.

10 If the web sites of pro-abortion groups are accurate, obtaining two signatures at private abortion clinics is not difficult (see, for example, www.mariestopes.org.uk).

11 The law in Scotland and Northern Ireland differs.

12 Office for National Statistics, Abortion Statistics 1998 and 1999, Series AB Nos 25 and 26, www.statistics.gov.uk. Figures and percentages for 1998 are very similar to 1999.

13 Section 1, subsection 2.

14 Quoted, Kerslake, *op cit*, p 169.

15 The Rawlinson Report found 87% of women surveyed had long-term emotional problems following abortion (p 29). Obtaining hard data here (even designing control studies) is problematic, and the evidence from numerous studies into post-abortion injury is not uniform. However, varying but significant levels of distress, guilt, lowered self-esteem, suicidal ideation and attempts, etc, are reported repeatedly in research studies. The precise risk of post-abortion trauma is unknown; that there *is a* risk seems clear.

16 Pro-abortion groups complain that we do *not* have abortion on request. However, the Marie Stopes organization state that, 'If you decide to have an abortion, then you are entitled to have ready access to counselling and a safe, legal abortion service such as ours' (www.mariestopes.org.uk). The National Abortion Campaign complain on their web site that 'Over a third of women are forced to skip the NHS process and pay for private abortions where it can be guaranteed that they will see two sympathetic doctors within an hour' (www.gn.apc.org/nac/uk_law.html). So abortion on demand *is* available, usually on the NHS, certainly privately.

17 See Paul Swope, 'Abortion: A Failure to Communicate,' in *First Things* 82, April 1998, pp 31-35.

18 Swope, p 35.

19 Richard Hays points out that it is precisely the ability to limit our love to some and not other neighbours that is ruled out by Jesus' parable of Good Samaritan. 'Who is *not* my neighbour?' is the question Jesus disallows, and this—Hays argues—applies to unborn neighbours too (Hays, *op cit*, p 451).

20 This dynamic also places out of sight and mind the issue of responsibility in entering into a sexual relationship in the first place, which is also part of our problem.

21 Meilaender, *Bioethics for Christians*, p 20.

22 In requests for abortion, *patients* tell their doctor whether their condition constitutes an illness to be cured or not, and specify the treatment they require. In other areas of medicine, that is bad practice.

23 Note the case of a woman from North-East England currently suing the NHS for not warning her of the distress she could suffer after having an abortion (reported on "Today," Radio 4, 12 June 2002. See http://news.bbc.co.uk/hi/english/health/newsid_2038000/2038823.stm). This is exactly the point that must be made. If we do not know the precise psychological risks of abortion, but have numerous studies indicating anything from a small to a very large incidence of post-abortion trauma, we must accept that there is a health risk to women in having an abortion. The question is how grave that risk is.

24 Anecdotally, GPs report that many women who reject a child through abortion soon choose to conceive a new child, whom they do keep. We should ask a lot of questions about this phenomenon.

25 On abortion being wrong because we are to welcome children, see Stallsworth (ed), *op cit*, especially the contributions by Willimon and Hauerwas.